SNIGLETS

RICH HALL & FRIENDS

Illustrated by Arnie Ten

MAGNOCARTIC *(mag no kar' tik)* n. Any automobile that, when left unattended, attracts shopping carts.

SNIGLETS

(*snig' lit*):
any word that doesn't appear in the
dictionary, but should

Collier Books • Macmillan Publishing Company • New York

"Not Necessarily the News," a production of Not the Network Company, Inc., in association with Moffitt-Lee Productions, is produced by John Moffitt and co-produced by Pat Tourk Lee.

Macmillan Publishing Company
866 Third Avenue, New York, N.Y. 10022
Collier Macmillan Canada, Inc.

Library of Congress Cataloging in Publication Data

Hall, Rich, 1954-
Sniglets (snig' lit): any word that doesn't appear
in the dictionary, but should.
1. Words, New—English—Anecdotes, facetiae, satire,
etc. 2. Vocabulary—Anecdotes, facetiae, satire, etc.
I. Title.
PN6231.W64H3 1984   428.1'0207   84-1883
ISBN 0-02-012530-5

10   9

Designed by Antler & Baldwin, Inc.
PRINTED IN THE UNITED STATES OF AMERICA

For Pat Tourk Lee and Jessica Tourk

CONTRIBUTORS

Todd Adamson Randy S. Alton Masey Amara Michele Amendola Brian and Jennie Barber Mark Belden Dave Bertschy Seth Bishop Sarah and Tracy Blossom Rick Boehm Andrea Breare Anthony Brown Valerie Burrgart Nancy Burt George Cahlik Rob Caldwell Susan Cargen Chuck Carter Tracy Carter Bart Cassel Melissa Cazel David Chapman Kim Chicken Elissa Cohen B. Conover Patrick Coughlin Marshall Deacon Brian DeMoss Chuck DeVaughn Patricia Dowding Rachel Drury Bryan Duke D'Laine Dury Jill Dyer Nancy C. Edlund Mark Eisenburg Karen Elliot Ron Ferraro Dennis Frizie Sean Gallagher John Garazzi Chris Griffin **Rich Hall** Zoe Hall Stuart E. Hallett III Jimmy Halliday Wanda Harkins David Harrington Staci Haynes John L. Henderson III Scott Henderson Mike Herdon Michael L. Hofmann G. R. Howard Louis Hubbell James P. Humphrey Jim Inskeep Katrina Jameson Alice Johnson Damon Jones Rob Kamm Barbara Kansas Diana Kent Jeff Koob Lance Krystopher Kristin Kulak Teresa Lamke Jeff Lange Tammy Lauper Mary Lauzon Rick Lubben Rick Luttenberger R. A. MacDonald Edmund Marcantonio Jed Martinez Meredith Maslanka Randi McDonald Scott McDonald Andrea McFarland Yvonne McHale Jonathan McKee Tom Menchyk Billy and Kelly Merton Cheri Lynn Monahan Dave Moran Mike and Apryl Moran Kevin Morgan Betty Morlan Roger Nalevanko Pat Nash Dave Nolan M. Nuckols Annice O'Brien Karen O'Byrne Michaelin Otis John Palatano Eric R. Pfeffinger Kevin Phillips Gerry Picard Charles A. Pluta Melinda Pofahl Tom Poisseroux Rick Powell Randall Putala Rob Ramsey Lucinda Reph George E. Reynolds III Mary T. Ritenburg Schatzie Schaefers Jenny Schoen Andy Schumacher Lynne Schuman Mike Sharp Bob and Bonnie Simko Annie Singer Darrell E. Smith Paula D. Smith Tisha Smith Pam Soule Kathy Spear Russell Spiler, Jr. B. Starkweather Tawnya Steinbrecher John Stempa, Jr. Debbie Swiz Stephen Szczesuil Jerry Tapp Sean Templeton Trey Terry Anne Tessari Gerald Tidman Guy Torak Jessica Tourk Jim Tursi Jody Uchtmann Mike Upton Ashland Vaughn Joe Vigil Jr. Renee Werbonski Sean Watt Dee Webster Ramona M. Weeks Brenda Wegmann Matthew Weiss Kay Well Maridee Whitehead Byron S. Winchester, Jr. Brian Yetter and Vincent Hurley Randy L. York Jodi Zahler John M. Zelenak Julian Zelizer

CONTENTS

ABZOT
(ab' zaht)

n. The device in a currency changer that determines whether a bill is too wrinkled or not.

ACCORDIONATED
(ah kor' de on ay tid)

adj. Being able to drive and refold a road map at the same time.

AEROMA
(ayr oh' ma)

n. The odor emanating from an exercise room after an aerobics workout.

AEROPALMICS
(ayr o palm' iks)

n. The study of wind resistance conducted by holding a cupped hand out the car window.

ALPONIUM
(al po' nee um)

n. (chemical symbol: Ap) Initial blast of odor upon opening a can of dog food.

AMBIPORTALOUS
(am bih port' ahl us)

adj. Possessing the uncanny knack for approaching a set of double doors and *always* pushing the locked one.

ANACEPTION
(an a sep' shun)

n. The body's ability to actually affect television reception by moving about the room.

ANTALIXIC
(ant a lik' sik)

n. One who passes over licorice jellybeans.

ANTICIPARCELLATE
(an ti si par' sel ate)

v. Waiting until the mailman is several houses down the street before picking up the mail, so as not to appear too anxious.

AQUADEXTROUS
(ak wa deks' trus)

adj. Possessing the ability to turn the bathtub faucet on and off with your toes.

AQUALIBRIUM
(ak wa lib' re um)

n. The point where the stream of drinking fountain water is at its perfect height, thus relieving the drinker from (a) having to suck the nozzle, or (b) squirting himself in the eye.

ARACHNIDIOT
(ar ak ni' di ot)

n. A person, who, having wandered into an "invisible" spider web begins gyrating and flailing about wildly.

ATTRINYL
(a try' nil)

n. (chemical symbol: At) A black, bulletproof, totally inflexible type of plastic, used primarily in covers of pay phone directories.

BANDILE
(ban' dyl)

n. The thin red strip one pulls to release a Band-Aid.

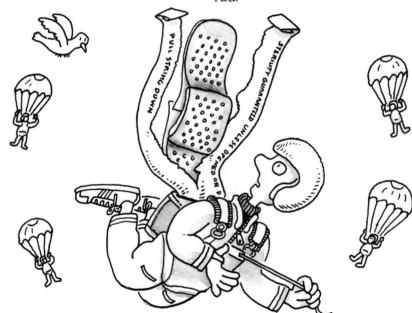

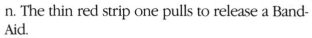

BARGARCS
(bar' jarks)

n. The streaks on a car's windshield from faulty wipers.

BATHQUAKE
(bath' kwake)

n. The violent quake that rattles the entire house when the water faucet is turned to a certain point.

BEVAMETER
(bev' a meet uhr)

n. (a unit of measure) The distance a coaster, attached to the bottom of a wet glass, will travel before it falls back to earth.

BLEEMUS
(blee' mus)

n. The disgusting film on the top of soups and cocoa that sit out for too long.

BLIBULA
(blib' byu luh)

n. The spot on a dog's stomach which, when rubbed, causes his leg to rotate wildly.

BLINDELIZE
(blin' dul eyes)

v. To scratch an album beyond recognition trying to maneuver it over the record spindle.

BLITHWAPPING
(blith' wap ing)

v. Using anything BUT a hammer to hammer a nail into the wall, such as shoes, lamp bases, doorstops, etc.

BLIVETT
(blib' vit)

v. To turn one's pillow over and over, looking for the cool spot.

BLOTCH
(blahch)

v. To slap the bottom of a catsup bottle with increasing intensity, ultimately resulting in BLOTCHSLIDE.

BOBBLOGESTURE
(bah blo jes' cher)

n. The classroom activity of not knowing an answer but raising one's hand anyway (after determining a sufficient number of other people have also raised their hands, thus reducing the likelihood of actually being called on).

BOSLUM
(bahz' lum)

n. The small metal ring on a ballpoint pen that separates the top half (MELANEXUS) from the bottom half (MOOSTERUS).

BOVILEXIA
(bo vil eks' e uh)

n. The uncontrollable urge to lean out the car window and yell "Moo!!" every time you pass a cow.

BRATTLED
(brat' uld)

adj. The unsettling feeling, at a stoplight, that the busload of kids that just pulled up beside you is making fun of you.

BRIMPLET
(brim' plit)

n. A frayed shoelace that must be moistened to pass through a shoe eyelet.

BUCKLINT
(buck' lint)

n. The fine red and blue threads running through new dollar bills.

BUCULETS
(buk' u lets)

n. The bumper guards on the underside of a toilet seat.

BUMPERGLINTS
(bump' ur glintz)

n. The small reflective obstacles in the middle of interstate highways which supposedly keep drivers awake and on the track.

BURBULATION
(ber byu lay' shun)

n. The obsessive act of opening and closing a refrigerator door in an attempt to catch it before the little automatic light comes on.

BURSPLOOT
(ber' sploot)

v. To position one's thumb at the end of a garden hose to increase the water pressure.

BUSBLENDER
(bus' blen dur)

n. The device at the front of the bus that tosses your fare around for awhile, then swallows it.

CABNICREEP
(kab' nih kreep)

n. The structural condition in which the closing of one kitchen cabinet causes another to open.

CAREENA
(ka reen' uh)

n. Any mangled or missing piece of highway guard rail.

CARPERPETUATION
(kar' pur pet u a shun)

n. The act, when vacuuming, of running over a string or a piece of lint at least a dozen times, reaching over and picking it up, examining it, then putting it back down to give the vacuum *one more chance*.

CEREOALLOCATIVE
(ser e o al'o ka tuv)

adj. Describes the ability of a seasoned breakfast eater to establish a perfect cereal/banana ratio, assuring there will be at least one slice of banana left for the final spoonful of cereal.

CHALKTRAUMA
(chawk' traw ma)

n. The body's reaction to someone running his fingernails down a chalkboard.

CHARP
(charp)

n. The green, mutant potato chip found in every bag.

CHEEDLE
(chee' dul)

n. The residue left on one's fingertips after consuming a bag of Cheetos.

CHOCONIVEROUS

(chahk o niv' ur us)

adj. The tendency when eating a chocolate Easter bunny to bite off the head first.

CHWADS
(chwadz)

n. The small, disgusting wads of chewed gum commonly found beneath table and counter tops.

CIGADENT
(sig' a dent)

n. Any accident involving a cigarette: for instance when it sticks to your lips while your fingers slide off and get burned.

CINEMUCK
(si' ne muk)

n. The combination of popcorn, soda, and melted chocolate which covers the floors of movie theaters.

CIRCLOCRYOGENIC THEORY
(sur klo kri o jen' ik   the' uh ree)

n. Postulates that no matter which way you turn a glass of ice water, the cubes will move to the back. (Further research has established that one piece of ice will always stick to the bottom of an empty glass until tapped, at which point it will come forward and smack the drinker on the end of his nose.)

CIRCULOIN TECHNIQUE
(sur' kew loyn   tek neek')

n. The popular approach to steak dining in which one eats around the edges first, then works his way toward the middle.

CLUMFERT
(klum' furt)

n. The invisible extra step at the top and bottom of a staircase. Usually materializes when one is carrying a large bag of groceries.

COEGGULANT
(ko eg' yu lent)

n. The white things in a plate of scrambled eggs.

CONAGRAPHS
(kohn' a grafs)

n. The raised relief squares on an ice cream cone.

CREEDLES
(kre' dulz)

n. The colony of microscopic indentations on a golf ball.

CRUMMOX
(krum' oks)

n. The cereal that gets caught between the inner lining and the side of the box. Also, the leftover amount at the bottom. (Not enough to eat, but too much to throw away.)

CURBSWELL
(kerb' swel)

n. A seismic condition in which the curb on the passenger side of a car will rise and wedge a car door. The passenger must then climb out and stand on the curb until the swelling goes down.

DASHO
(da' show)

n. The area between a car's windshield and dashboard, where coins, pencils, etc. cannot be humanly retrieved.

DETERRENCY
(de ter' ren see)

n. The ruined currency found in pants pockets after laundering.

DETRUNCUS
(de trunk' us)

n. The embarrassing phenomenon of losing one's bathing shorts while diving into a swimming pool.

DISCONFECT
(dis kon fekt')

v. To sterilize the piece of candy you dropped on the floor by blowing on it, somehow assuming this will "remove" all the germs.

DOOR SLINKY
(dor   slin' kee)

n. The springy device attached to the back of a door that prevents the door from marring the wall.

DUBLECTATE
(duh blek' tayt)

v. To misplace one's eyeglasses and eventually discover them atop one's head.

ECNALUBMA
(ek na lub' ma)

n. A rescue vehicle which can only be seen in the rear-view mirror.

ELBONICS
(el bon' iks)

n. The actions of two people maneuvering for one armrest in a movie theater.

ELECELLERATION
(el a cel er ay' shun)

n. The mistaken notion that the more you press an elevator button the faster it will arrive.

EQUATT
(e' kwat)

n. The pastime of trying to balance the light switch in the exact middle of the wall plate, so that the light is half on, half off.

ERDU
(uhr' dew)

n. The leftover accumulation of rubber particles after erasing a mistake on a test paper.

ESCALASTICIZE
(esk a last' i size)

v. To lean against the rail of a moving escalator and have the sensation of being pulled in opposite directions.

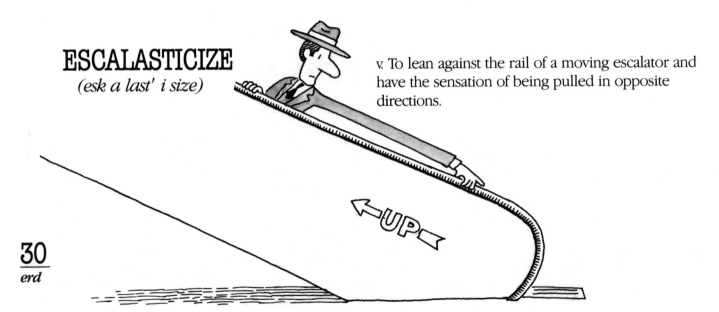

EUNEEBLIC
(you nee' blik)

n. A person who refuses to believe an "out of order" sign and risks his money anyway.

EXPRESSHOLES
(eks pres' holz)

n. People who try to sneak more than the "eight items or less" into the express checkout line.

FENDERBERG
(fen' dur burg)

n. The large glacial deposits that form on the insides of car fenders during snowstorms.

FLANNISTER
(flan' is tur)

n. The plastic yoke that holds a six-pack of beer together.

FLEN
(flen)

n. (chemical symbol: Fl) The black crusty residue that accumulates on the necks of old catsup bottles.

FLEPTIC
(flep' tik)

adj. The tendency of soup and dog food lids to slip into the can upon opening.

FLIRR
(flur)

n. A photograph that features the camera operator's finger in the corner.

FLOLES
(flolz)

n. The extra (fourth and fifth) holes in notebook paper. Created in the hopes that one day mankind will perfect a "five ring binder."

FLOPCORN
(flop' korn)

n. The unpopped kernels at the bottom of the cooker.

FLOTION
(flo' shun)

n. The tendency when sharing a waterbed to undulate for five minutes every time the other person moves.

FLOTTA FACTOR
(flah' ta fak' tur)

n. The proven scientific fact that at a self-service pump, the last ten cents take longer to reach the tank than the first twelve dollars' worth.

FLOWFRIGHT
(flo' frite)

n. The desperate attempt by a homeowner to "talk" his overflowing toilet into backing down.

FLUGGLING

(flug' ul ing)

v. The dangerous practice, in a darkened room, of using one's finger to guide the end of an electrical plug into a wall socket.

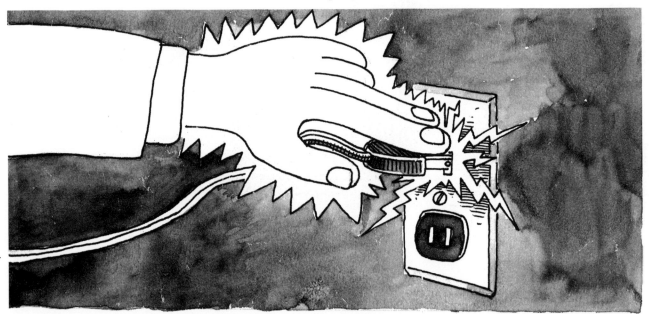

FRAZNIT
(frahs' nit)

n. Any string hanging from an article of clothing, which when pulled causes the article to completely unravel.

FRUST
(frust)

n. The small line of debris that refuses to be swept onto the dust pan and keeps backing a person across the room until he finally decides to give up and sweep it under the rug.

FURBLING
(fer' bling)

v. Having to wander through a maze of ropes at an airport or bank even when you are the only person in line.

FURNIDENTS
(fer' nih dents)

n. The indentations that appear in carpets after a piece of furniture has been removed.

FURTERUS ZONE
(fer ter' us   zohn)

n. The empty stretches of bun on either end of a hot dog.

GARMITES
(gar' mitz)

n. Those items of clothing that fit perfectly in the store, but somehow shrink on the way home.

GENDERPLEX
(jen' dur pleks)

n. The predicament of a person in a theme restaurant who is unable to determine his or her designated bathroom (e.g., turtles and tortoises).

GERTATIOUS
(gur tay' shus)

adj. Having the adolescent fear that hanging one's arm over the bed at night will mean being dragged under.

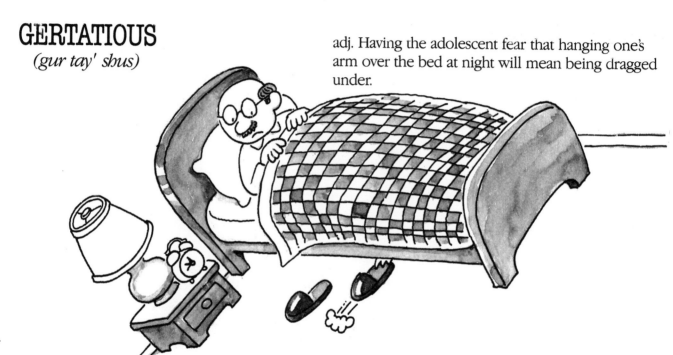

GLACKETT
(glak' it)

n. The noisy ball inside a spray-paint can.

GLADHANDLING
(glad' han dling)

n. To attempt, with frustrating results, to find and separate the ends of a plastic-sandwich or trash bag.

GLANTICS
(glan' tiks)

n. Two people, who, while making out, open their eyes at the same time to see if the other is looking.

GLEEMULE
(glee' mule)

n. (a unit of measure) One unit of toothpaste, measured from bristle to bristle. (Not to be confused with GLEEMITES, which are petrified deposits of toothpaste found in sinks.)

GLUTETIC CHAIR
(glew tet' ik   chair)

adj. A twentieth-century design of chair, found most often in movie theaters. The main feature of the Glutetic chair is its ability to keep folding up underneath a person as he tries to force it down with his rear.

GRACKLES
(grak' elz)

n. The wrinkles that appear on the body after staying in water too long.

GREELITE
(gree' lite)

n. The eerie glow that emanates from beneath escalator steps.

GRINION
(grin' yun)

n. The unsightly indentation in the middle of a belt when it has been worn too long.

GRIPTION
(grip' shun)

n. The sound of sneakers squeaking against the floor during basketball games.

GRISKNOB
(gris' nahb)

n. The end of a chicken drumstick which always gives the appearance of having more chicken on it.

GURMLISH
(gurm' lish)

n. The red warning flag at the top of a club sandwich toothpick which prevents the person from biting into it and puncturing the roof of his mouth.

HANGLE
(han' gul)

n. A cluster of coat hangers.

HEMPENNANT
(hem' pen ent)

n. Any coattail, cuff, or dress hem dangling outside the door of a moving vehicle.

HOZONE
(ho' zohn)

n. The place where one sock in every laundry load disappears to.

HUDNUT
(hud' nut)

n. The bolt left over when one has finished reassembling a bicycle or car engine.

HYDRALATION
(hi dra lay' shun)

n. Acclimating oneself to a cold swimming pool by bodily regions: toe-to-knee, knee-to-waist, waist-to-elbow, elbow-to-neck.

HYSTIOBLOGINATION
(his' te o blahg in ay' shun)

n. The act of trying to identify a gift by holding it to your ear and shaking it.

IDIOT BOX
(id' e ot bahks)

n. The part of the envelope that tells a person *where* to place the stamp when they can't quite figure it out for themselves.

IGNISECOND
(ig' ni sek und)

n. The overlapping moment of time when the hand is locking the car door even as the brain is saying "my keys are in there!"

JIFFYLUST
(ji' phee lust)

n. The inability to be the first person to carve into a brand-new beautiful jar of peanut butter.

KEDOPHOBIA
(ked oh fo' be uh)

n. The fear of having one's sneakers eaten by the teeth on the escalator.

KNIMPEL
(nim' pul)

n. The missing last piece of a jigsaw puzzle.

KROGT
(kraht)

n. (chemical symbol: Kr) The metallic silver coating found on fast-food game cards.

LACTOMANGULATION
(lak' to man gyu lay' shun)

n. Manhandling the "open here" spout on a milk carton so badly that one has to resort to using the "illegal" side.

LAMINITES
(lam' in itz)

n. Those strange people who show up in the photo sections of brand-new wallets.

LOTSHOCK
(laht' shahk)

n. The act of parking your car, walking away, and then watching it roll past you.

LUB
(lub)

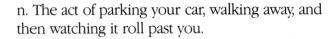

n. The small deposit of spinach that lodges itself between one's teeth.

McMONIA
(muk moan' ee uh)

n. (chemical symbol: Mc) Noxious gas created by fast-food employee mopping under your table while you're eating.

MAGGIT
(mag' it)

n. Any of the hundreds of subscription cards that fall from the pages of a magazine (pl. MAGGREGATE).

MAGNIPHOBIA
(mag ni fo' be uh)

n. The fear that the object in the side mirror is *much much* closer than it appears.

MANGLAZETTE
(mang la zet')

n. The newspaper at the top of the stack that everyone passes over, believing the ones beneath it have better or fresher news.

MARP
(marp)

n. The impossible-to-find beginning of a roll of cellophane tape.

MATTRESCOTTING
(mat' res kot ing)

n. The pattern of gray and white lines on an institutional mattress.

MAYPOP
(may' pahp)

n. A bald tire.

MEMNANTS
(mem' nents)

n. The chipped or broken *m&m's* at the bottom of the bag.

MERFERATOR
(mur' fur ay ter)

n. The cardboard core in a toilet tissue roll.

METHYLPHOBIA
(meth il fo' be uh)

n. The fear that you are going to have to pay for the one cent you over-pumped at the self-service station.

MITTSQUINTER
(mit' skwint ur)

n. A ballplayer who looks into his glove after missing the ball, as if, somehow, the cause of the error lies there.

MOPHENES
(mo' feenz)

n. The semi-truck headlights that invade your motel room at three in the morning.

MOTSPUR
(mot' sper)

n. The pesky fourth wheel on a shopping cart that refuses to cooperate with the other three.

MOWMUFFINS
(mo' muh finz)

n. The dried accumulation of grass on the underside of lawnmowers.

MUMPHREYS
(mum' freez)

n. (a useless sniglet) Those strange extra digits you find on push-button phones.

MUSQUIRT
(mus' kwirt)

n. The water that comes out of the initial squirts of a squeeze mustard bottle.

MUSTGO
(must' go)

n. Any item of food that has been sitting in the refrigerator so long it has become a science project.

NAPJERK
(nap' jurk)

n. The sudden convulsion of the body just as one is about to doze off.

NIZ
(niz)

n. An annoying hair at the top of a movie screen.

OATGAP
(oht' gap)

n. The empty space in a cereal box created by "settling during shipment."

OPLING
(oh' pling)

n. The act, when feeding a baby, of opening and closing one's mouth, smacking one's lips and making "yummy" noises, in the hope that baby will do the same.

OPTORTIONIST
(op tor' shun ist)

n. The kid in school who can turn his eyelids inside out.

OROGAMI
(or oh ga' mee)

n. The miraculous folding process that allows Kleenexes to methodically emerge from the box one at a time.

OROSUCTUOUS
(or oh suk' chew us)

adj. Being able to hold a glass to one's face by sheer lung power.

PEDIDDEL
(pe did' ul)

n. A car with only one working headlight. (*Related to* LEDDIDEP: a car with only one working taillight.)

PEDLOCK
(ped' lahk)

n. The condition of a bicycle pedal wedging itself against the kickstand.

PELP
(pelp)

n. The crumbs and food particles that accumulate in the cracks of dining tables.

PENCIVENTILATION
(pen si ven ti lay' shun)

n. The act of blowing on the tip of a pencil after sharpening it.

PERCUBURP
(per' kyu berp)

n. The final gasp a coffee percolator makes to alert you it is ready.

PETRIBAR
(pet' ri bar)

n. Any sun-bleached prehistoric candy that has been sitting in the window of a vending machine too long.

PETROOL
(pet' rul)

n. The slow, seemingly endless strand of motor oil at the end of the can.

PEWTONE
(pyu tone')

n. (chemical symbol: Pu) A major atmospheric component of towns with paper mills.

PHISTEL
(fis' tul)

n. The brake pedal on the passenger side of the car that you wish existed when you're riding with a lunatic.

PHONESIA
(fo nee' zhuh)

n. The affliction of dialing a phone number and forgetting whom you were calling just as they answer.

PHOSFLINK
(fos' flink)

v. To flick a bulb on and off when it burns out (as if, somehow, that will bring it back to life).

PHOTOYOKEL
(fo to yo' kul)

n. A person who presses the wrong button on a film camera causing it to dismantle.

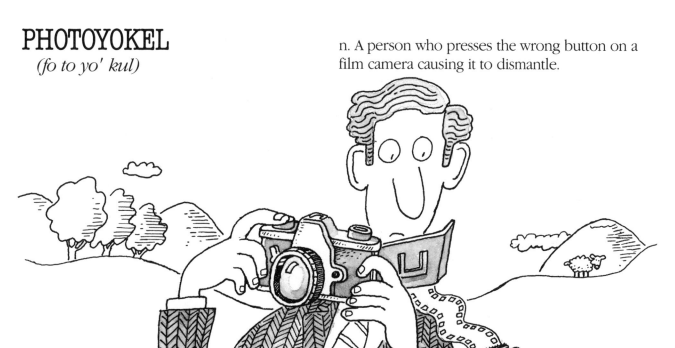

PHOZZLE
(fo' zul)

n. The buildup of dust on a record needle.

PICKLETTULANCE
(pik ul et' yu lans)

n. The ability to remember the entire family's order at a fast-food restaurant.

PIFFLESQUIT
(pif' ul skwit)

n. The wire net surrounding the cork of a champagne bottle.

PILLSBURGLAR
(pilz' berg ler)

n. Person able to sample the icing on a new cake without leaving a fingerprint.

PIYAN
(pi' an)

n. (acronym: "Plus If You Act Now") Any miscellaneous item thrown in on a late night television ad. (Example: a pitchman trying to sell an all purpose carving knife . . . "it's the only knife you'll ever need. Plus if you act now, this complete set of steak knives . . .")

POINT BLIMFARK
(poynt blim' fark)

n. The point at which the wheels on a stagecoach appear to turn in the opposite direction.

PORKUS NON GRATIS
(por' kus non grat' is)

n. The scraggly piece of bacon at the bottom of the package.

PREMBLEMEMBLEMATION
(prim blum em blum ay' shun)

n. Whenever you drop a letter in the mailbox, you always re-check to make sure it's gone down.

PROFANITYPE
(pro fan' i tipe)

n. The special symbols used by cartoonists to replace swear words (points, asterisks, stars, and so on). It is yet to be determined which specific character represents which specific expletive.

PSYCHOPHOBIA
(sy ko fo' be uh)

n. The compulsion, when using a host's bathroom, to peer behind the shower curtain and make sure no one is waiting for you.

PUPKUS
(pup' kus)

n. The moist residue left on a window after a dog presses its nose to it.

PURPITATION
(per pi tay' shun)

v. To take something off the grocery shelf, decide you don't want it, and then put it in another section.

RETROCARBONIC
(ret ro kar bon' ik)

n. Any drink machine that dispenses the soda before the cup.

RICEROACH

(rys' rohch)

n. The burnt krispie in every bowl of Rice Krispies.

RIGNITION
(rig ni' shun)

n. The embarrassing action of trying to start one's car with the engine already running.

ROCKTOSE
(rok' tohs)

n. The hard lumps that block the pouring spouts of sugar dispensers.

ROVALERT
(ro' val urt)

n. The system whereby one dog can quickly establish an entire neighborhood network of barking.

RUBUNCLES
(ru' bunk ulz)

n. The bumps on an uncooked chicken.

SARK
(sark)

n. The marks left on one's ankle after wearing tube socks all day.

SCADINK
(ska' dink)

n. The annoying buildup of ink on the end of a ball-point pen.

SCANDROIDS
(skan' droydz)

n. The striped price codes which mysteriously began appearing on consumer products a few years ago.

SCHLATTWHAPPER
(shlat' wap ur)

n. The window shade that allows itself to be pulled down, hesitates for a second, then snaps up in your face.

SCHNUFFEL
(shnuf' ul)

n. A dog's practice of continuously nuzzling your crotch in mixed company.

SCRIBLINE
(skrib' line)

n. The blank area on the back of credit cards where one's signature goes.

SCRIT
(skrit)

n. Anything that's been in the same place for at least fifty years without being used, such as the archaic bottles of hair tonic on a barber's counter.

SHIRTLOP
(shurt' lahp)

n. The condition of a shirt that has been improperly buttoned.

SHOEFLY
(shew' fliy)

n. The aeronautical terminology for a football player who misses the punt and launches his shoe instead.

SHUGGLEFTULATION
(shug lef tuyl ay' shun)

n. The actions of two people approaching, trying to get around each other, and muttering "thanks for the dance."

SIRLINES
(sir' lines)

n. The lines on a grilled steak.

72 SLACKJAM
sho   *(slak' jam)*

n. The condition of being trapped in one's own trousers while trying to pull them on without first removing shoes.

SLOOPAGE
(slu' paj)

n. The tendency of hot dogs, hamburgers, and sandwich contents to slip from between their covers.

73
slo

SLOTGREED
(slot' greed)

n. The habit of checking every coin return one passes for change.

SLURM
(slerm)

n. The slime that accumulates on the underside of a soap bar when it sits in the dish too long.

SLUTURES
(slew' chers)

n. The four white threads that protrude from Levis after the tag has been removed.

SNORFING
(snorf' ing)

n. The little game waitresses love to play of waiting until your mouth is full before sneaking up and asking, "Is everything okay?"

SPAGMUMPS
(spag' mumps)

n. Any of the millions of Styrofoam wads that accompany mail-order items. (*Also,* SPAGBULLIONS: custom fitted Styrofoam blocks that accompany stereo equipment.)

SPECLUMS
(spek' lums)

n. The miniscule bumps on a strawberry.

SPERAWS
(sper' awz)

n. The pinched marks on the ends of hot dogs.

SPIBBLE
(spib' ul)

n. The metal barrier on a rotary phone that prevents you from dialing past 0.

SPIROBITS
(spy' ro bits)

n. The frayed bits of left-behind paper in a spiral notebook.

SPIRTLE
(spur' tul)

n. The fine stream from a grapefruit that always lands right in your eye.

SPORK
(spork)

n. The combination spoon/fork you find in fast food restaurants.

SPRATCHETT
(spra' chit)

n. The rubber bar at a checkout counter that separates one load of groceries from another.

SPUBBLING
(spub' ling)

v. The superhuman feat of trying to wash one's hands and manipulate the "water saving" faucets at the same time.

SQUALKEENUS
(skwal ke' nus)

n. The shock syndrome that comes from biting into a popsicle with one's front teeth.

SQUATCHO
(skwatch' oh)

n. (another useless sniglet) The button at the top of a baseball cap.

STROODLE
(stru' dul)

n. The annoying strand of cheese stretching from a slice of hot pizza to one's mouth.

STRUMBLE
(strum' bul)

n. That invisible object you always pretend made you trip, when it was actually your own stupid clumsiness.

STURP
(sterp)

v. To pin down a runaway piece of paper or currency with one's foot before the wind blows it away.

SUBNOUGATE
(sub new' get)

v. To eat the bottom caramels in a candy box and carefully replace the top level, hoping no one will notice.

SUCCUBEEBISH
(suk yu be' bish)

n. The gelatinous substance found surrounding canned hams and Vienna sausages.

SUPERFLUHOLES
(sup ur flew' holz)

n. (another useless sniglet) The phony holes on speaker covers, put there to match the ones that actually surround the speaker.

TELECRASTINATION
(tel e kras tin ay' shun)

n. The act of always letting the phone ring at least twice before you pick it up, even when you're only six inches away.

TELEPRESSION
(tel e pre' shun)

n. The deep-seated guilt which stems from knowing that you did not try hard enough to "look up the number on your own" and instead put the burden on the directory assistant.

THERMALOPHOBIA
(thur muh lo fo' be uh)

n. The fear when showering that someone will sneak in, flush the toilet, and scald you to death.

THERNOT
(ther' nut)

n. The cardboard rod on a hanger that prevents creasing in pants.

THRICKLE
(thri' kel)

n. The itch in the back of the throat which can't be scratched without making disgusting barnyard-type noises.

TIEFRIGHT
(ty' fryt)

n. The fear that no matter which way you turn the twist-tie on a loaf of bread, it is the wrong direction.

TILE COMET
(tyl kom' it)

n. Any streamer of toilet paper attached to your heel as you emerge from a public restroom.

TIREQUILLS
(tyr' kwils)

n. The small rubbery protrusions on new tires.

TOASTATE
(tohs' tayt)

v. To impatiently pop toast up and down in the toaster, thus increasing the likelihood of burning it.

TOLLOAF
(toe' lohf)

v. Act of missing a toll basket and having to climb out of your car to retrieve the coin.

TRITZ
(trits)

n. The holes in saltine crackers.

TWINCH
(twinch)

n. The movement a dog makes with its head when it hears a high-pitched noise.

UFLUATION
(yu flu ay' shun)

n. The peculiar habit, when searching for a snack, of constantly returning to the refrigerator in hopes that something new will have materialized.

UHFAGE
(uff' aj)

n. The unit for determining a television's age, that is, the amount of time it takes for the picture to appear once the set has been turned on.

UPULS
(yu' puls)

n. The blank pages at the beginning and end of books, presumably placed there so you can rewrite the ending.

VULCANT
(vul' kant)

n. (chemical symbol: Vu) The stale air that emanates from a flat tire.

WARBLOID
(war' bloyd)

n. The tiny device in cassette players that eats tapes.

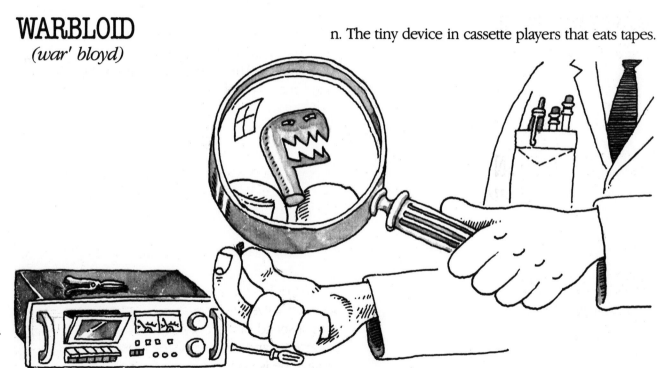

WATTBOBBLE
(wat' bah bul)

v. To remove a hot light bulb by turning it several seconds, letting your fingers cool, then repeating the process. This is generally followed by the glorious revelation of using your shirttail.

WERXILATION
(wurks ul ay' shun)

n. The property of some screen doors to start to slam shut only to catch themselves at the last moment and "float" to a gentle close.

WILY'S LAW
(wi' leez law)

n. The only known exception to Newton's Law of Gravity, Wily's Law states that an animal or person can suspend himself in midair provided (a) he is in a cartoon, and (b) he doesn't look down and realize he is no longer on solid ground.

WONDRACIDE
(wun' druh side)

n. The act of murdering a piece of bread with a knife and cold butter.

WURBLET
(wer' blit)

n. The line of moisture on one's trousers that comes from leaning against a wet counter in a public restroom.

##

n. Any word formed when typewriter keys jam together.

XIIDIGITATION
(ksi dij i tay' shun)

n. The practice of trying to determine the year a movie was made by deciphering the roman numerals at the end of the credits.

YARDRIBBONS
(yard rib' onz)

n. The unmowed patches of grass discovered after one has put away the mower.

YINKEL
(yin' kul)

n. A person who combs his hair over his bald spot, hoping no one will notice.

ZIBULA
(zi' bew luh)

n. The plastic spine which model car parts come attached to.

ZIMETER
(zi' me tur)

n. (a unit of measure) The last four or five inches of tape measure that never rewind automatically.

ZIPPLE
(zi' pul)

n. A broken poptop on a beer or soda can.

ZIZZEBOTS
(zi' ze botz)

n. The marks on the bridge of one's nose visible when glasses are removed.

ZYXNOID
(ziks' noyd)

n. Any word that a crossword puzzler makes up to complete the last blank, accompanied by the rationalization that there probably is an ancient god named Ubbbu, or German river named Wfor, and besides, who's going to check?

Anatomical Sniglets

CHINGRIP *(chin' grip)* n. Area where chin meets neck. Used for holding pillow when slipping on pillowcase.

GIMPLEXUS *(gim plek' sis)* n. Rear area of thighs, which must be peeled from car seat on hot summer days.

GLARPO *(glar' po)* n. The juncture of the ear and skull where pencils are stored.

GNARMBLUM *(narm' blum)* n. The dry wrinkly area at the end of the elbow.

GROMAXES *(grom' ack sis)* n. Inside area of knees used to grip steering wheel when holding a road map.

NUGLOO *(nug' lew)* n. Single continuous eyebrow that covers entire forehead.

SCRABITCH *(skrab' ich)* n. Impossible-to-reach area in middle of back which can never be scratched.

SNIFFLERIDGE *(snif' ul rij)* n. Trough leading from the nose to upper lip.

SWAZNA *(swaz' nuh)* n. The thin, disgusting membrane that connects the bottom of the tongue to the top of the jaw, presumably to hold it in place.

YINK *(yinc)* n. One strand of hair that covers bald spot.

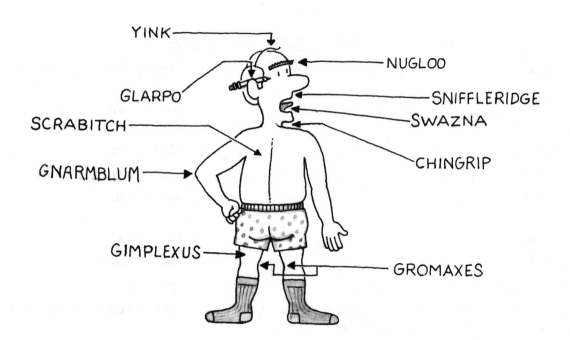

YINK

NUGLOO

GLARPO

SNIFFLERIDGE

SCRABITCH

SWAZNA

GNARMBLUM

CHINGRIP

GIMPLEXUS

GROMAXES

93

Extra Added Bonus Section for Poets

YORANGE
(yawr' anj)

n. Those disgusting white threads that hang from an orange after it has been peeled.

OFFICIAL SNIGLETS ENTRY BLANK

Dear Rich:

    Here's my sniglet, which is every bit as clever as any in this dictionary:

_____

_____

_____

_____

_____

Sincerely,

(name)   _____

(street address)   _____

(city, state, zip code) _____

SNIGLETS
P.O. Box 2350
Hollywood, CA 90078

NEVITTS
(nev' itz)

n. The sandpaper-like deposits on a cat's tongue.

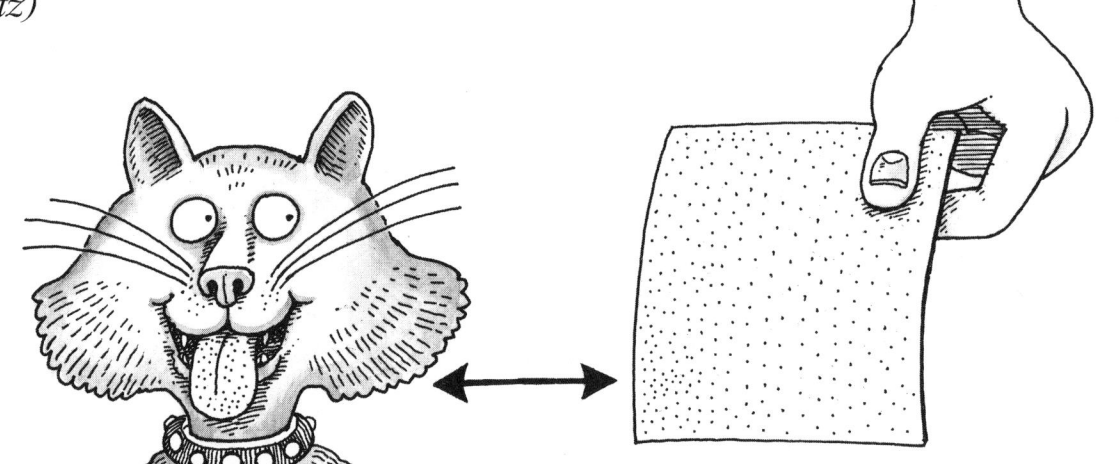

NISTOLS
(niz' tolz)

n. The small rubbery pads on the bottom of a dog's paw.

NERKLE (nur' kel)
n. A person who leaves his Christmas lights up all year.

NEONPHANCY (ne on' fan see)
n. A fluorescent light bulb struggling to come to life.

NEGLINTICS (ne glin' tiks)
n. The study of why dark lint attaches itself to light clothing and vice versa.

NARCOLEPTULACY (nar ko lep' ul ab see)
n. The contagious action of yawning, causing everyone else in sight to also yawn.